FUN TO MAKE AND DO

By **HANNAH TOFTS**
and **ANNIE OWEN**

Editor Diane James
Photography Jon Barnes

TWO-CAN

CONTENTS

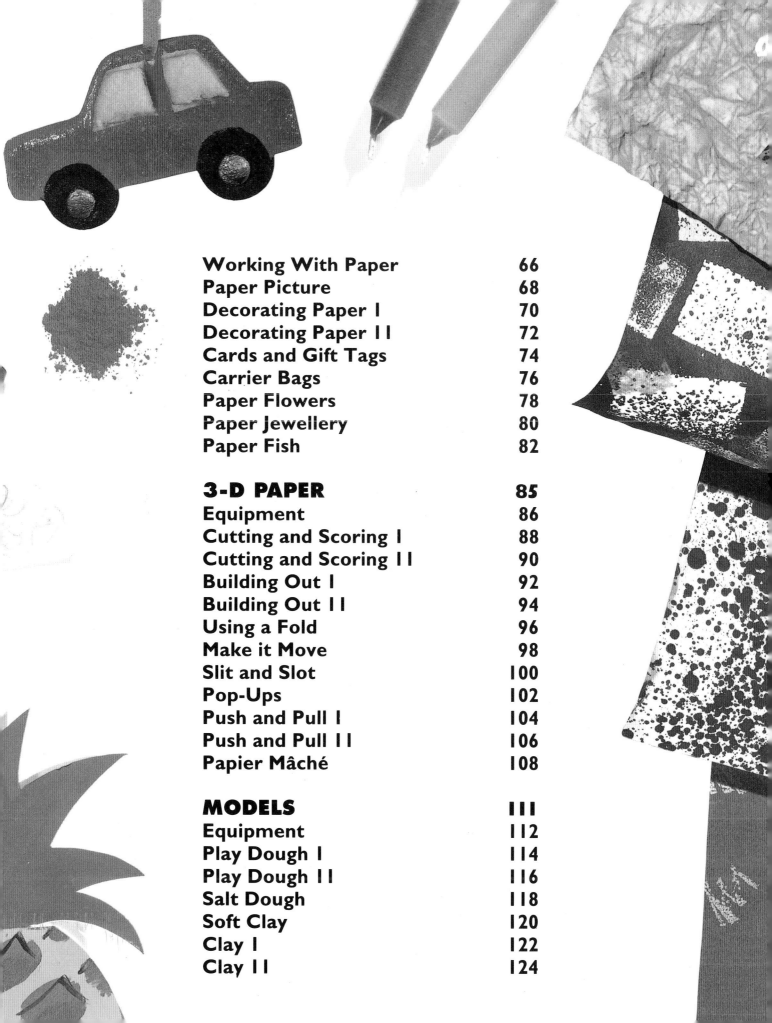

Published by
Two-Can Publishing Ltd
346 Old Street
London EC1V 9NQ

First edition 1990
Reprinted 1995

Colour Separation by Next Graphic Limited, Hong Kong.

Printed & bound by ORIENTAL PRESS, (DUBAI).

ISBN: 1-85434-400-5

PAINT

CONTENTS

EQUIPMENT

All of the things on these pages are used somewhere in the PAINT section. You should be able to find most of them in your house or at school but some you may have to buy from craft shops or toy shops.

Keep a look out for things that might be useful - plastic spoons, foil containers, plastic pots and scraps of fabric.

For most painting you can use poster, powder, water or ready-mixed paint. But for some things you will need special paints.

It is useful to have a selection of fat and thin brushes - short, stiff-ended brushes are good for stencilling and splattering.

Some painting can be extremely messy so keep a good supply of newspaper to put on the floor.

coloured candles

fabric paint pens

poster paint

fabric paint

poster paint

straws for splattering

fabric for decorating

small brushes

large pointed brush

bric paint

large flat brush

stencil brushes

WHISTLER 65

egg for decorating

string for printing

wax crayons

Mixing your own colours can be very satisfying. Although you may get muddy colours sometimes, they will certainly be different!

Try adding more and less water when you are mixing paints to give different effects.

Colour Mixing
Yellow + Red = Orange
Blue + Yellow = Green
Blue + Red = Purple

Look around the house for empty yoghurt pots, plastic trays and lids to mix paints in.

Keep your eyes open for useful brushes such as old toothbrushes, small scrubbing brushes and paint brushes. If no-one wants them, you can cut them down and use them for stencilling or splattering.

Try not to damage your brushes by being rough with them when you are mixing. Moving them in just one direction will keep the hairs smooth and make the brushes last longer.

BRITISH MADE
2½"

All the family can join in the fun of hand and feet painting! First put down plenty of newspaper because it can be very messy!

Cover the bottoms of your feet in fairly thick paint and make foot prints on a large sheet of paper. You should get an interesting effect and the paint will wash off afterwards.

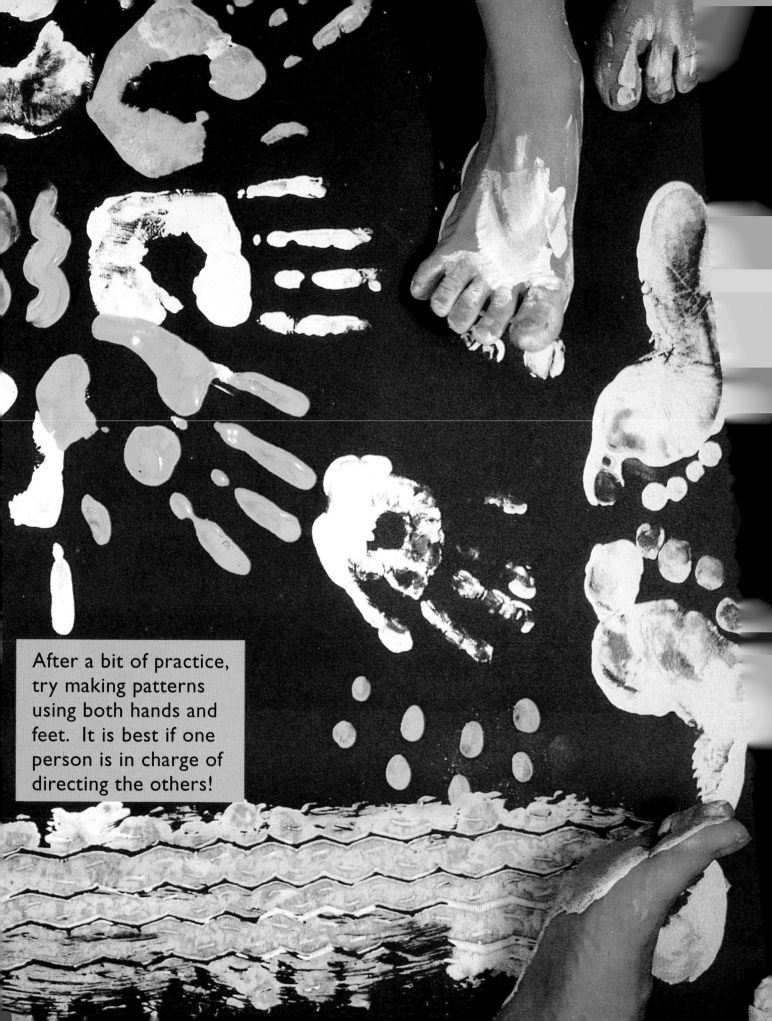

After a bit of practice, try making patterns using both hands and feet. It is best if one person is in charge of directing the others!

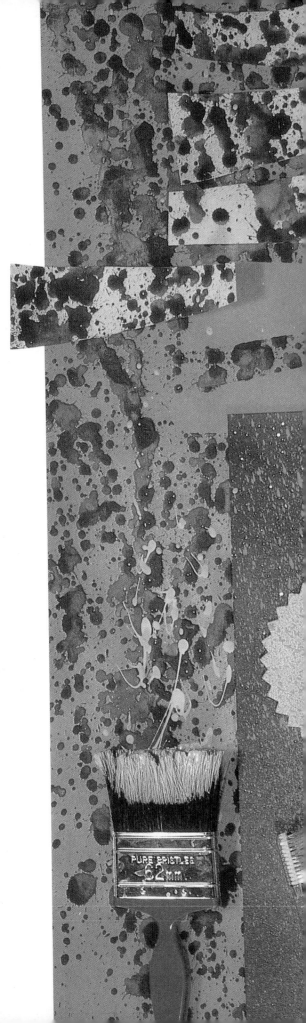

Straw Painting

Drip some runny paint on to a sheet of paper. Get close to the paint and blow gently through a straw. The paint should make strange patterns as it spreads across the paper.

If you use a different colour straight away, the colours will mix and blend together in places. If you don't want this effect, wait until the first colour is dry.

Splatter With Small Brushes

Find a selection of small brushes with short, stiff bristles such as an old toothbrush or a nail brush. Dip one of the brushes in medium thick paint. Hold the brush over a large sheet of paper and run a small piece of card down the bristles. You should get a fine speckled effect on the paper!

Try masking out areas by laying shapes of card on the clean paper. Splatter over the shapes. When you lift the card off, there will be a clear shape left behind!

Splatter With Large Brushes

Try to find the kind of paint brush normally used to paint walls. Dip it in medium thick paint. Stand over a large sheet of paper and flick the brush up and down. You should get an interesting effect of large speckles! Try using different colours on top of each other.

All of these methods are very messy so make sure all surfaces are well covered.

MIRROR PRINTS

▽ Fold a large sheet of paper in half. Unfold the paper and drop some fairly runny paint along the fold and on either side of the fold. Fold the paper over along the original fold and smooth it over with your hand. You can use just one colour or several different colours. If you don't want the colours to run together, allow each colour to dry before you drop on blobs of the next colour.

▲ Fold a sheet of paper in half and then open out flat again.

Dip some lengths of string in some runny paint and lay them on one side of the paper with the ends hanging over the edge.

Try to make interesting shapes with the string.

Fold the paper over along the original fold and smooth over with your hand.

Put your left hand firmly on top of the folded paper and pull the ends of the string out with your right hand.

Unfold the paper and you will find two swirly patterns.

If you don't want the colours to mix together, lay one piece of string down at a time and allow the paint to dry before using the next colour.

▶ Wax and paint do not mix but you can get some interesting effects by using them together. Make some simple patterns on a sheet of paper with a wax crayon. Paint over the pattern with some runny paint. The paint will not stay where the wax marks are!

▼ Look for something that has an interesting texture – the bark of a tree or piece of rough wood. Tape a piece of paper over the textured surface and carefully rub with a wax crayon.
  Paint over the wax pattern with some runny paint.

▶ Draw a picture or make a pattern with wax crayons. Using a thick brush and fairly runny black paint, cover the whole picture. The wax crayons will show through leaving a black background to your picture.

▼ Colour a sheet of paper with different coloured wax crayons – there shouldn't be any white paper showing! Paint over the wax with thick black paint – you may need several layers – and leave to dry.
  Scrape some of the paint away with the back of a spoon or the end of a pencil. The wax crayon will show through where you scrape the paint away.

Try making patterns with raw vegetables and paint! Look for vegetables with interesting textures.

Start with a carrot. You can slice the carrot across the middle or lengthwise. Dip the cut surface in some thick paint and press on to a sheet of paper.

Cut a potato in half. You can either scoop out a pattern in the cut surface or, using a knife, cut away a section to leave a raised pattern. Dip the potato halves in thick paint and print on to paper. A cabbage cut in quarters also makes a good print.

Try experimenting with other vegetables cut in different ways.

Paste Recipe

1 Measure out a mug of flour and 3 mugs of water.

2 In a saucepan, mix a little of the water with the flour to make a smooth paste.

3 Add the rest of the water and ask a grown-up to heat the mixture until it boils – they must keep stirring all the time! Turn the heat down and let the mixture simmer until the paste thickens.

You can make some interesting patterns with paste paint. When the paste is cold, spoon a little into some small containers. Add some paint to each and mix well.

Cut out pieces of cardboard to use as scrapers. Try making notches in the end of one piece to give an interesting shape.

Cover a piece of paper with paste paint using a thick brush. Using card scrapers, scrape away areas of the paste paint. Try making different marks by using different sizes of scrapers.

By now, you should have lots of patterns and pictures that need framing! Or you might want to make frames for your postcards and photographs.

First cut some frames from pieces of cardboard. Make sure that the inside of the frame is slightly smaller than the picture you want to frame.

If you start with a small frame and then glue a larger one on top then a slightly larger one on top of that, you will get a stepped effect.

Try using some of the methods like splattering, wax and paint and paste paper to decorate your frames.

If you want to use paste paper, glue the paste paper on to the card before you cut out the frame.

STENCILLING

You can buy special stencil card from craft shops, but ordinary card works as well.

You will also need a craft knife, a stencil brush with short, stiff hairs and some thick paint.

Draw some simple shapes on to a piece of stencil card. Cut the shapes out with a craft knife, but ask for help if you haven't used one before.

You can stencil on to most surfaces – paper, card, fabric and wood. But it is best to try your idea out on paper first.

Hold the stencil down firmly with one hand and stipple the paint on – inside the stencil – with a stencil brush.

You can use different colours but allow each colour to dry first before using the next.

Not all Easter eggs are made of chocolate! These eggs have been hard-boiled and decorated with wax crayons, candle wax, food colouring and onion skins!

Always ask for help when boiling the eggs and make sure they are cold before you decorate them.

Treat the eggs gently when you are decorating them or they will crack!

Onion Skin Eggs

Wrap an egg in layers of onion skins. Put the egg and skins on to a piece of fabric or into the toe of a pair of tights and tie up the parcel! Hard-boil the egg. When the water is cool take the egg out and unwrap it. It will be beautifully marbled in an orange-brown colour.

Wax and Dye Eggs 1

Draw a pattern on an egg – before hard-boiling – with a white wax crayon or a piece of candle. Don't press too hard!

Put a few drops of food colouring into some water in a saucepan and hard-boil the egg. When the egg is cooked, take it out and leave it to cool. The food colouring colours the egg in the places where there is no wax.

Wax and Dye Eggs 2

Ask a grown-up to hard-boil an egg and help with dripping the wax on.

Light a candle and let blobs of wax drop on to the egg. Put some food colouring and water into a saucer and gently roll the egg around. Drop some more candle wax on to the egg and roll it in darker food colouring and water.

Put the egg in a medium hot oven for a few minutes. Take the egg out and wipe off any excess wax. These eggs are for decoration only!

The plates, knives, forks and spoons on the tablecloth may look real, but you can't pick them up because they are painted on.

If you use special fabric paints and pens – from craft shops – you can wash the fabric over and over and the paint won't come out!

It helps to put a piece of card under the area you are painting to keep the material steady.

Fabric pens are good for doing outlines and detailed work but use the paints and a fat brush for larger areas.

Most fabric paints should be left to dry and then ironed but always read the instructions carefully.

Marbling is not difficult to do and you can use marbled papers for writing on or for wrapping presents or covering books. Every sheet will look different!

Find a baking tin at least 2.5 cm (1 inch) high and large enough to hold the size of paper you want to marble.

Fill the tin almost to the top with water and add a few drops of vinegar.

Drop small amounts of any oil-based paint on to the surface of the water and swirl them around with a stick, pencil or cardboard comb.

Hold opposite ends of a clean sheet of paper and lay it on the surface of the water. Try to make sure there are no air bubbles. Gently lift the paper off and put it – coloured side up – on some newspaper to dry.

Turn over the page and see how many different effects you can get. Try taking more than one print from the same paints.

PRINT

CONTENTS

EQUIPMENT

Here are some of the things you will need to start printing. Almost anything with a raised surface will give a print so look for different textures.

You can use almost any paint for printing but oil paint gives the best results. If you use oil paint you will need a good supply of rags and turpentine for cleaning up.

Look for flat surfaces to roll your paint on to for printing – lino or the shiny side of a piece of hardboard are best.

Be very careful when using a craft knife – ask for help if you have problems with cutting! Always use a piece of thick card or lino to cut on.

block of wood

tape

craft knife

card and paper

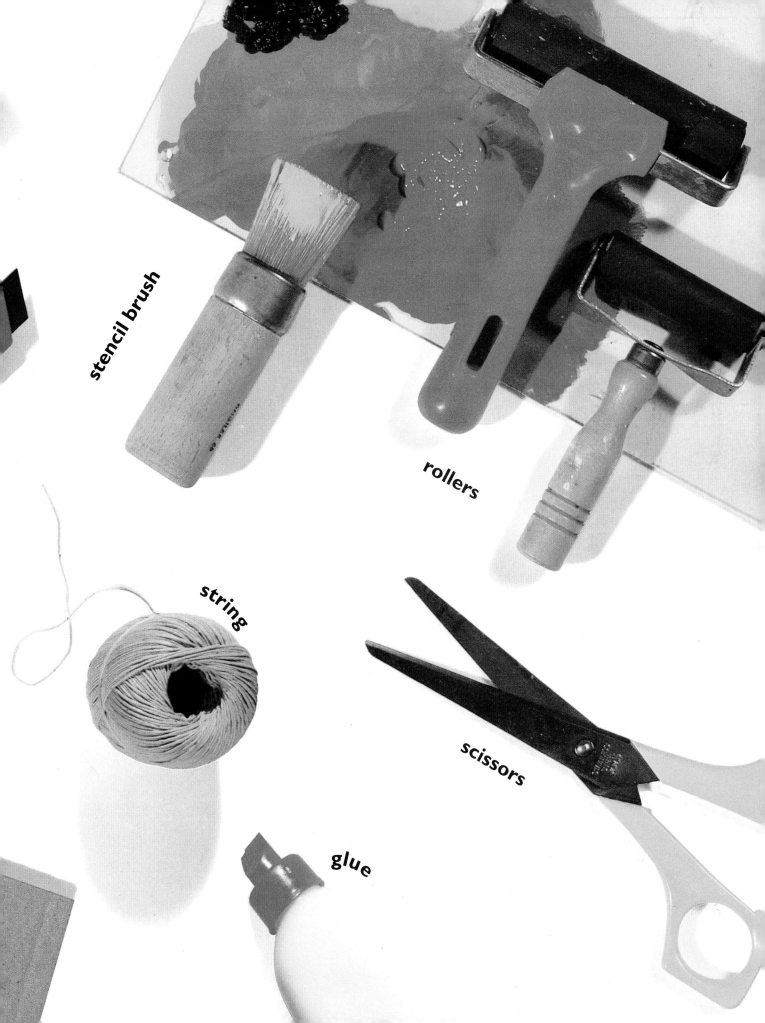

stencil brush

rollers

string

scissors

glue

You can take a print from most things that have a textured surface – rough, knobbly or patterned. Look around both indoors and outdoors for different textures.

You will have to cover the object that you want to take a print from with paint. Make sure you will not be doing any permanent damage and, if in doubt, use paint that will wash off easily.

Use thick paint and a large brush or roller to cover the surface you want to print from. Lay a sheet of paper over the object and press down firmly and smoothly or run a clean roller over the paper. Lift the paper off gently and leave your print to dry. Try experimenting by combining different textures.

The prints above were made from a rough plank of wood, a car tyre and a manhole cover. The ones on the left were made with blocks of wood and leaves.

Here are some suggestions for making simple printing blocks that you can use over and over again.

Using an old rolling pin, wrap string round and round and glue the ends firmly. Mix some fairly thick paint on a piece of lino or hardboard (shiny side). Roll the rolling pin up and down the paint to coat the string. Make a print by rolling the rolling pin smoothly along a piece of paper.

You can make other printing blocks by gluing string on to a block of wood in a pattern. Or, you can wind thick cord round a block, or stick on lengths of broken pasta. Try taking more than one print before covering the block with paint again.

Think of ways you could use
your printed papers – wrapping
paper, covering books or even
as wallpaper!

These printing blocks are easy to make and give good, strong prints.

Use pieces of thick card for the printing blocks. From another piece of card, cut straight strips. Glue the strips onto the printing block to make a pattern.

Cover the printing block with fairly thick paint using a roller. Press the block firmly on to a sheet of paper and smooth over with a clean roller.

Try using strips of torn paper or thin card instead of straight strips. Make two or three blocks in the same way but use different colours of paint to print each one. See how many different patterns you can make by alternating the colours.

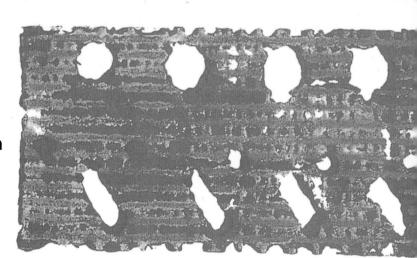

These printing blocks are made by cutting shapes out of pieces of card. Cut two rectangles from an old cardboard box using a craft knife. Ask a grown-up to help.

Cut shapes from one of the pieces of card – diamonds, triangles, squares and rectangles. Cover the card with fairly thick paint and make a print. Now, cut shapes out of the other piece of card. You will be printing this piece of card on top of the first print, so try to use shapes that will work well. Use a different colour to print the second block on top of the first.

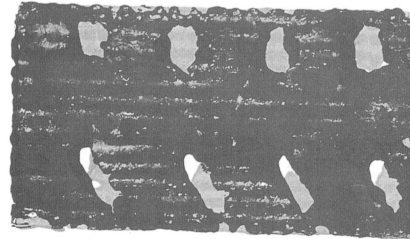

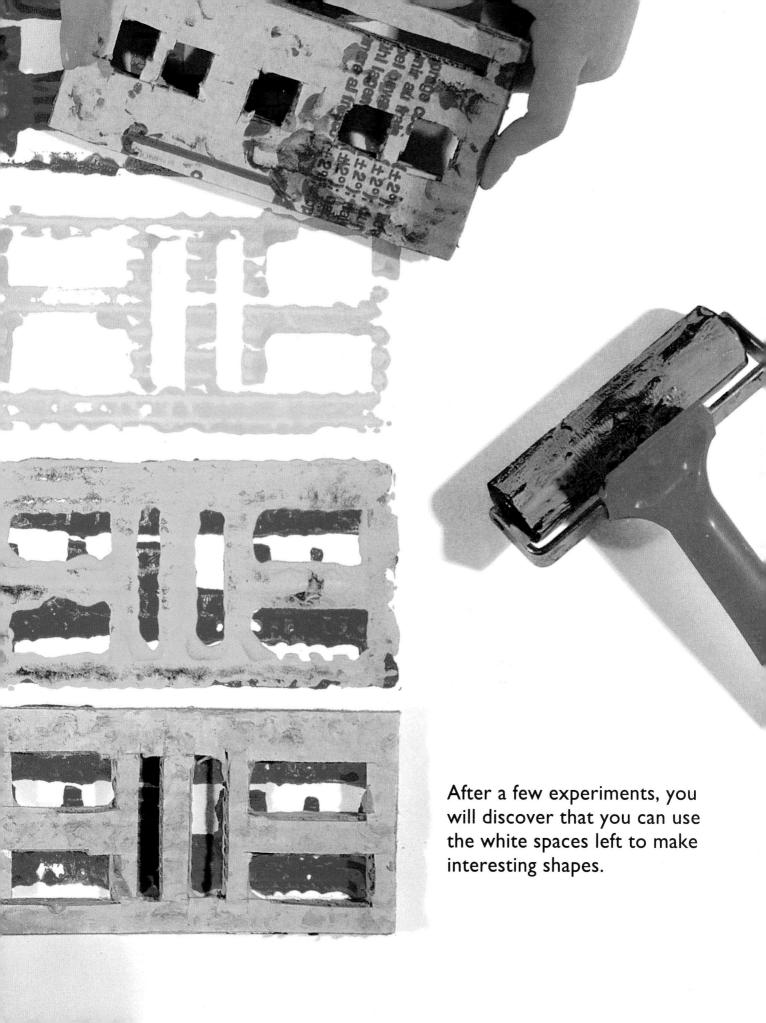

After a few experiments, you will discover that you can use the white spaces left to make interesting shapes.

Here is a method for making several prints of the same picture. First, make a colour drawing and then trace it.

Cut a separate piece of card – the same size as your trace – for each colour that you want to use. Lay your traced drawing on one of the pieces of card and trace off all the objects that are the same colour. Do the same for each colour on separate pieces of card. Now trace all the objects onto a separate sheet of card and cut them out. Glue the card shapes in position on the sheets of card. These are your printing blocks.

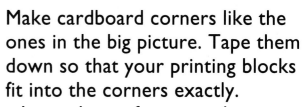

Make cardboard corners like the ones in the big picture. Tape them down so that your printing blocks fit into the corners exactly.

Lay a sheet of paper – the same size as the printing blocks – in the card corners. Roll paint over one of the printing blocks. Place it carefully over the sheet of paper using the card corners as a guide. Press down and lift off. Repeat this process with each of the different colours.

Try building up a picture using printed shapes! Cut shapes from stiff card using a craft knife. Ask a grown-up to help. Use a strip of card as a handle. Fold it in half and bend back the two ends. Stick the ends firmly to the back of your card shapes. Cut up old cardboard tubes and use the edges to print curves. Use thick paint and watery paint to get different effects. Try overprinting shapes while they are still wet.

STENCIL AND SPLATTER

To make a stencil, see page 26. Place the stencil on a sheet of paper and use a stencil brush – with short, stiff hairs – to stipple the paint on.

You can use the shape cut from the stencil to make a print. Lay the shape on a piece of paper and splatter paint over it (see page 14). Use a nail brush or an old toothbrush and a piece of card to splatter with. Always splatter away from you!

Try making this pattern by laying card rectangles on a piece of black paper and stippling over them with white paint. Re-position the rectangles and stipple over with yellow paint.

Try experimenting with different shapes to build up your own patterns.

You can make a print using a flat surface. This is called monoprinting. You need a smooth surface such as a piece of lino or hardboard (shiny side). Some kitchen table tops can be used but make sure the paint will wash off afterwards.

To make a pattern like the one above, cover the flat surface with fairly thick paint. Use a piece of card to scrape away patterns from the paint. Lay a sheet of paper carefully over the pattern. Smooth the paper gently with your hand. Peel the paper back to reveal your print! Try making more than one print.

Another method of monoprinting is to paint a simple picture straight on to your flat surface. Lay a sheet of paper over the picture and smooth over carefully. Lift the paper off and leave the print to dry.

Try printing a picture for your wall! You can use lots of different printing methods in the same picture but keep the shapes as simple as possible. Start with the background and build the picture up.

Patterns make good pictures too! Look at the leaf pattern here and try to work out your own patterns using different printing blocks and stencils.

Here are some examples of printed papers using methods from this section. Try making a selection of your own designs. You can use printed paper to cover books, to write on, to wrap presents and as pictures for your wall!

Try making your own writing paper! You can print border designs using simple shapes and you can personalise the paper by printing your name on it! If you want to print your name or initials, try using very simple shapes to make letters. Turn the page and you will find some suggestions for printing your own envelopes.

PAPER

CONTENTS

BY AIR MAIL
PAR AVION
MIT LUFTPOST

Offres Meublés 4e

MARAIS 5.500 F
2 P cft. 42.25.32.25

MARAIS GD LUXE
45.26.11.24

RESIDENCE
PRES PORTE DE BERC
DE 4 JOURS À 1 MOIS
STUDIOS - CUIS. EQUIPEE
TEL. TV. MENAGE. PARKING
2-3-4 PERSONNES. 1er PRIX
200 F/JOUR MOIS — 10 %
GANDOLFI (1) 48.83.04.69

PORTE DE VINCENNES
résidence 22, rue de la Voute
nombreux studios meublés, ft
équipement qua-

ÉTOILE
PARFAITEMEN
CALME 3.600

USAirmail

You don't have to buy expensive paper to make any of the things in this section. Look at all the different papers on these pages. Now look around your house and see what you can find – old wrapping paper, brown paper, the insides of envelopes, corrugated card used for packing, used stamps, postcards, cereal packets, sweet wrappers and old newspapers.

Later on, you will find lots of different ways to decorate plain paper. Start making a collection of different papers now!

EQUIPMENT

When you have gathered together a collection of different papers, you are almost ready to start! All of the things on these pages are used somewhere in the PAPER section, for cutting, gluing, decorating and assembling. You will probably be able to find most of them in your house but you may have to buy some of them from craft or toy shops.

Remember: be very careful when using scissors and craft knives – ask for help if you have any problems with cutting and always use a piece of thick card or lino when you are cutting with a sharp knife.

straws for splattering and decorating

ruler for straight lines

scissors

paint and brushes for decorating paper

cocktail sticks for flower stems

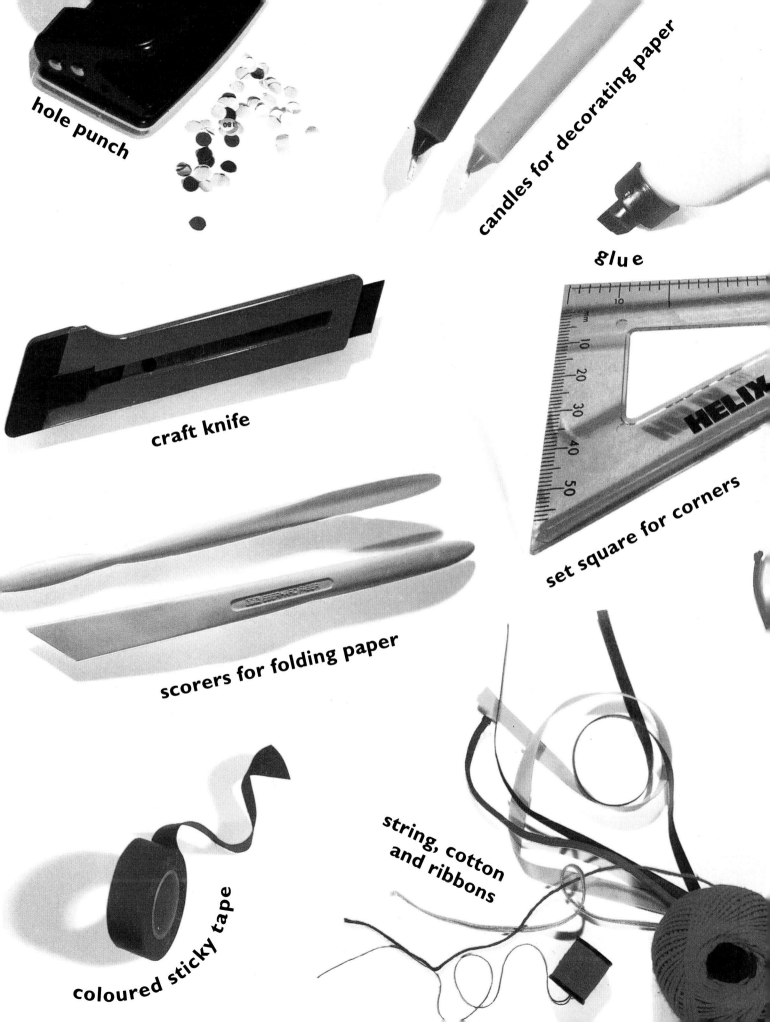

hole punch

candles for decorating paper

glue

craft knife

set square for corners

scorers for folding paper

string, cotton
and ribbons

coloured sticky tape

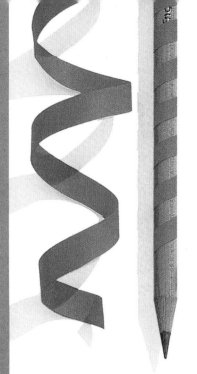

Paper Curls

Cut a long, thin strip of coloured paper. Wrap the strip tightly round a pencil or knitting needle. Pull the pencil or needle out and you will have a paper curl!

Paper Beads

Stick two sheets of coloured paper together. Tear out triangles and roll them up tightly, starting at the wide end.

Crumpled Paper

Give paper an interesting texture by crumpling it up. When you are collecting papers, look for paper that has already been crumpled up.

Weaving Paper

Cut out some long, thin strips of different coloured paper. Weave the strips in and out as in the picture. If you want the strips to stay in position, glue them on to a backing sheet.

Stick and Tear

You can make paper stronger by gluing two layers together. If you glue two different colours together and then tear out shapes, you will get an interesting edge. If you stick three or more layers of paper together, you will get an even stronger paper – more like thin card!

Concertina Folds

Take a long, thin strip of paper and practise making concertina folds or pleats. They can be as large or small as you like. Later on you will see how to use pleated paper to make jewellery and paper flowers.

Cutting, Punching and Tearing

Cutting paper gives a smooth edge while tearing leaves a ragged edge – both methods give interesting effects and are used in this section. If you have a hole punch, you can punch small round holes – keep the pieces, they may be useful!

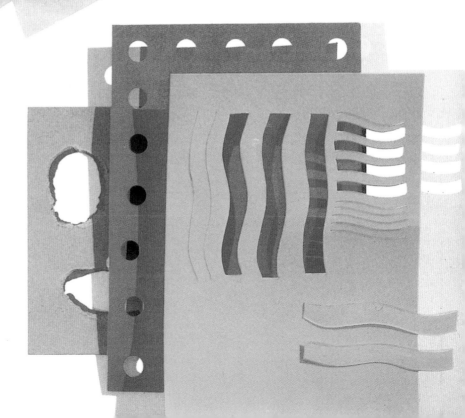

If you look carefully at this picture, you will see that it is made entirely from different papers.

Look around the house to see how many different kinds of paper you can find. The papers here include newspaper, insides of envelopes, brown paper, wrapping paper, greaseproof paper and tissue paper – there are also plastic straws and milk bottle tops!

Draw a rough sketch of your idea and decide which papers will be best
  Cut and tear the papers into shapes and stick them in position, starting with the background.
  Remember that you can bend, curl and crumple paper and card to make interesting shapes. Look at pages 66 and 67 to find out how to weave paper and make concertina folds.

Here are some examples of decorated papers using different methods.

Sponge Printing

Try dipping different shaped sponges – large and small – into fairly thick paint. Press the sponge on to the paper.

Object Printing

Look for objects that have an interesting shape or a raised texture. Dip the objects into fairly thick paint and press them on to the paper.

Wax and Paint

Make a pattern on the paper with wax crayons or candles. Paint over the wax marks with medium-thick paint. The paint will not stay where the wax marks are.

Crumpled Paper

Crumple up a small piece of paper and dip it into thick paint. Press it on to the paper to make a print.

Splattering

This is a very quick and easy method for decorating paper. Turn to page 14 to see how it's done.

Here are some more methods for decorating papers.

Experiment with the suggestions in this book and try out your own ideas too.

1 6 Splatter painting

2 9 Crumpled paper printing

3 Crumpled paper – paint a sheet of paper and scrunch it up

4 Sponge printing – try using different types of sponges

5 8 Paste paper – see page 22 for paste paint method

7 Wax and paint

10 Sponge and object printing

You don't need any paints or coloured pencils to make these cards and gift tags! All you need is coloured paper, glue, scissors and a craft knife. Ask a grown-up to help.

Slit and Slot Card

Fold a sheet of coloured paper in half. Make slits from the top to the bottom using a craft knife. Leave a border of at least 2.5 cm (1 inch) all round the card.

Using different coloured strips of paper, weave them in and out of the slits.

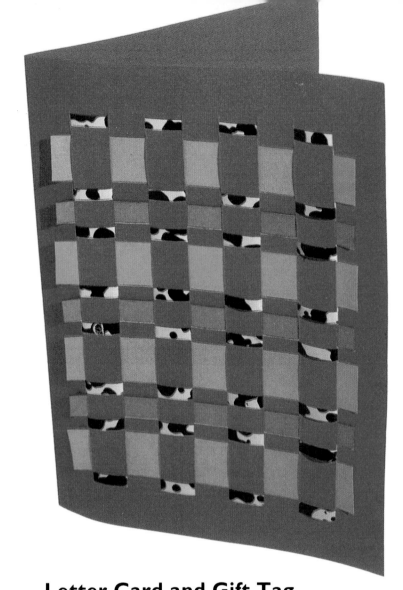

Letter Card and Gift Tag

Paste two sheets of different coloured paper together and fold in half. Using a craft knife, cut the shape of a letter from the front of the card. Keep the letter that you cut out and punch a hole in it. Thread a piece of cord through the hole and you will have a gift tag!

Punch and Tear Card

Paste two sheets of different coloured paper together and fold in half to make a card. Pierce holes in the front of the card with a pencil and tear back strips of paper to make a pattern.

Cut Paper Card

Fold a sheet of coloured paper in half. Using a craft knife, cut wavy slits and wavy shapes in the front of the card. Stick the shapes you cut out back on the front of the card.

Gift Tags

Cut triangles or other shapes from coloured paper. Punch holes in the tops of the triangles or shapes and thread a ribbon through. Write a message on the gift tag and attach it to a present!

First decide how big you want your carrier bag to be!

1 On the back of a sheet of decorated paper draw out a plan like the one at the top of the page. The pieces marked 'A' will be the sides of the bag and should be the same measurement. The pieces marked 'B' will be the front and back of the bag and these should also be the same measurement. The pieces marked 'C' should measure just less than the width of 'A'. The front and back pieces marked 'B' should be wider than the sides!

2 Cut out corners and triangles as shown on the illustration. Use a scoring tool to score all the lines marked. The height of the triangles to be scored – marked 'X'– should be equal to half the width of the sides of the bag – also marked 'X'.

3 Fold over and glue the top of the bag. This makes a strong, neat edge.

4 You can either use a hole punch to punch holes for cord at the top of the bag (front and back), or you can make small slits to thread ribbon through.

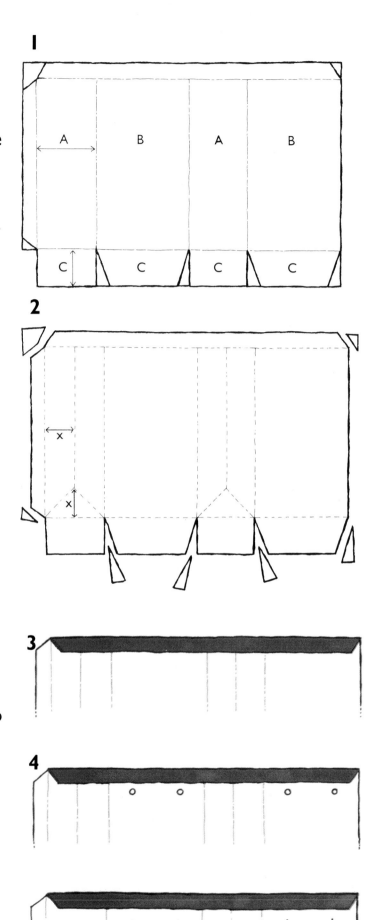

8 Slot cord or ribbon through the holes for handles.

5 Glue the bag together at the flap edge.

6 Fold the bottom flaps under and glue.

7 Gently push in the sides along the scored lines.

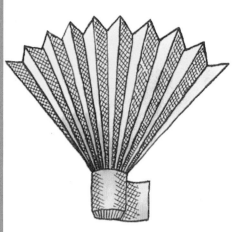

Here are some ideas for making paper flowers – try your own ideas too!

Pleat a strip of coloured paper, then pinch one end together and stick a strip of paper round to hold it.

Cut a long strip of coloured paper. Make cuts along the length as in the illustration. Roll up the paper and bend the petals back. Try using different coloured papers. Add leaves and stem.

To make stems for your paper flowers wrap a thin strip of green paper round a cocktail stick. Glue or tape the ends. Push the stem up into the middle of the flower and glue.

Stick flowers into yoghurt pots filled with sand.

Cut out different shapes for leaves – long and thin, short and pointed. Score down the centre of the leaf and fold. Leaves are good for covering up joins between flowers and stems!

This 'petal' flower was made by cutting separate coloured petals, overlapping them and sticking them together. The paper curls were made by wrapping thin strips of paper round a pencil.

Cut petal shapes in a long strip of paper as in the illustration. Roll the flower up and fold back the petals. Tissue paper makes good roses. Try making the petals different shapes.

Woven Earrings

Cut some thin strips of different coloured papers. Weave the strips in and out. When you have made a woven square, cut out a piece of paper the same size and glue them together. Glue an earring attachment to the back.

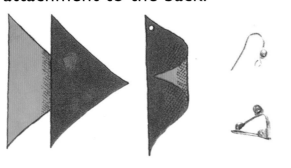

Triangle Earrings

Glue two different coloured triangles together. Curl the triangle round the handle of a wooden spoon. Pierce a small hole at the top of two triangles and thread an earring attachment through.

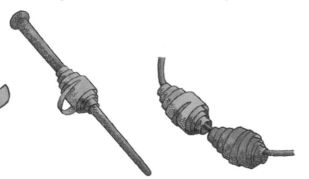

Paper Beads

Cut out a long, thin paper triangle. Starting at the wide end, roll the triangle round a knitting needle. Pull the needle out. Make a collection of beads and string them onto coloured cord.

Pleated Brooch

Cut out two paper triangles. Pleat the triangles like the ones in the illustration. Glue the long edges together. Pinch the pleats together in the middle. Wrap and glue a thin strip of paper round the middle to hold the pleats in place. Glue a brooch attachment to the back.

Concertina Bracelet

Take two long strips of paper. Glue the ends together at right angles. Continue folding one piece over the other as in the illustration. Glue the ends together. Because concertina folds stretch, you should be able to slip the bracelet over your wrist easily.

You should be able to find earring attachments in craft shops. You may also find hair slides which you can stick paper bows or flowers to.

These fish don't need feeding and you can make them any colour you like! If you can't find a goldfish bowl, an old fish tank or a large glass jar will work just as well. Look at the instructions on the next page.

Turn the container upside down on to a piece of card and draw round the edge. Cut out the shape. Use sticky tape to attach different lengths of cotton to the fish and to the cardboard top. Put the top over the bowl and watch your fish swimming around!

Cut some simple fish shapes out of coloured card. Using a craft knife, cut patterns in the fish or use a pencil to punch holes. Try sticking different coloured card behind the cut-out shapes.

You can make watery shapes by using the insides of envelopes, and strips of of curled paper make good seaweed!

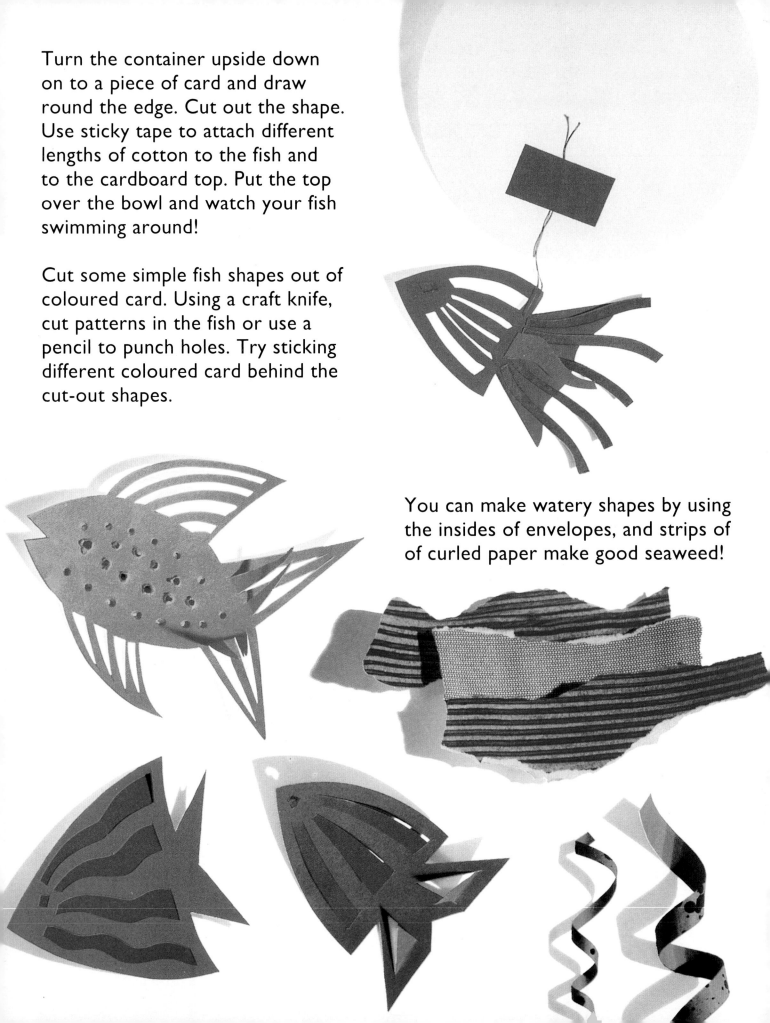

3-D PAPER

CONTENTS

EQUIPMENT

In this section you will find lots of different ways to make 3-D (three dimensional) shapes out of flat paper and card. Make a collection of empty packets and boxes, cardboard tubes and old egg cartons. Look for cardboard that has an interesting texture, such as corrugated card. Be very careful when using a craft knife. Ask for help from a grown-up and use a flat surface to cut on.

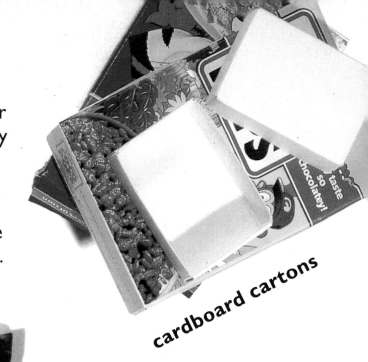

cardboard cartons

craft knife

cardboard tubes

collection of card and paper

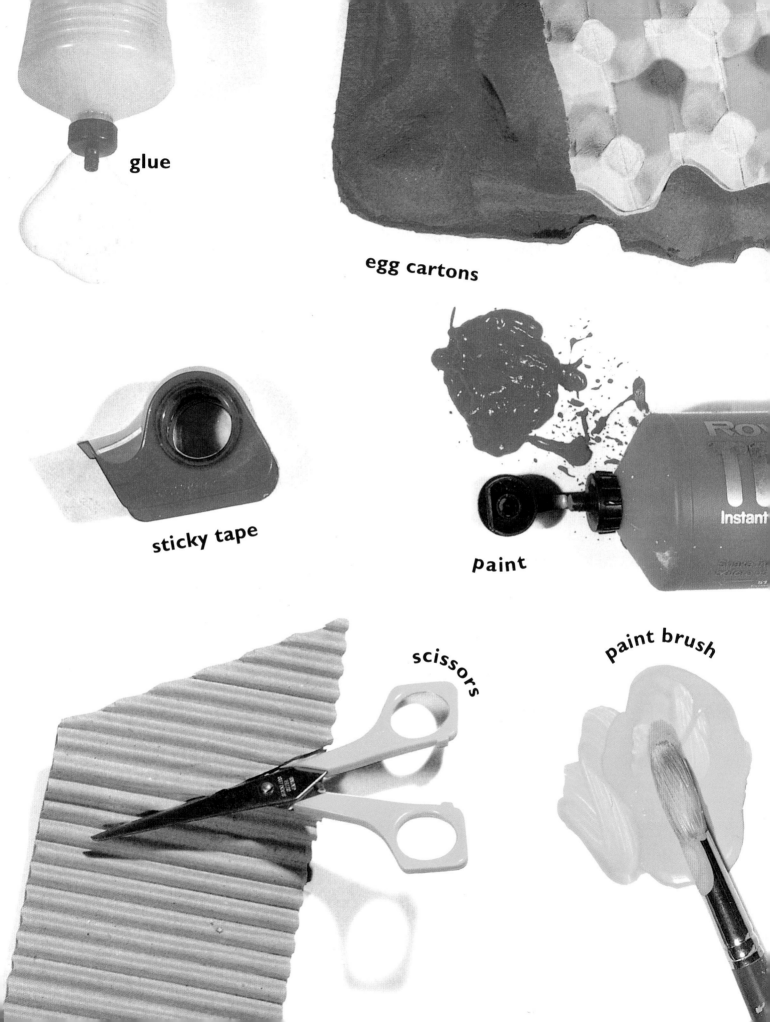

glue

egg cartons

sticky tape

paint

paint brush

scissors

Here are some suggestions for altering the shape of a flat piece of paper using simple cuts. Try cutting half squares, circles and triangles like the ones at the top of the picture. Fold back every other strip of paper.

To make the wavy triangles like the ones in the picture below, first score the wavy shapes on the paper. Cut triangles from one score line to the other. Fold the triangles upwards. Try scoring and cutting other simple shapes.

Try cutting wide strips out of the paper and rolling the ends round a fat pencil to make paper rolls.

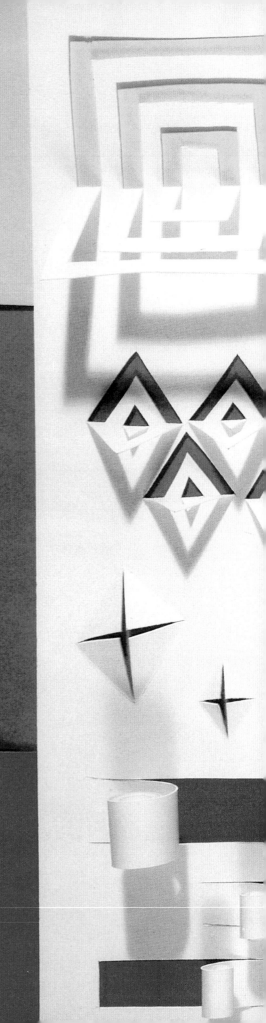

Be very careful when cutting with a craft knife.

Here are some more ideas for cutting and scoring using concertina folds (see page 67). Score straight lines down a sheet of paper or thin card using a ruler and a scoring tool. Make concertina folds along the score lines.

Use a pencil and ruler to draw squares or triangles in the centre of a fold. The picture below shows you how to do this. Score along the dotted lines and cut along the solid lines with a craft knife. Gently push the shapes up or down away from the fold.

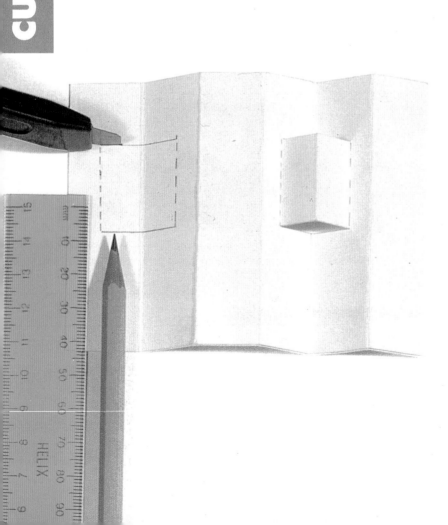

This picture was made simply by sticking card shapes on top of each other. First sketch out a rough design and work out how your layers will build up. Cut shapes from thick, soft card and paint them. Stick the shapes in position. Watch how the shapes begin to make shadows as they build up.

To make a 3-D picture like this one, you will need a good collection of interesting shapes. Look for lots of different boxes, tubes, cartons and packaging materials. Lay your collection out and play around with the shapes until you have a well-balanced pattern. Either paint the shapes before you stick them down or use spray paint afterwards.

Make your shapes stand up! Fold a sheet of card or stiff paper in half. Draw a shape on the card and cut round it. Do not cut along the fold or your shape will not stand up!

To make the dog shown here, you also need a head which is cut out separately. Leave a tab on the end to slot through a slit made in the body. The pineapple leaves were done in the same way.

When slotting shapes together, make sure that the slit is exactly the same length as the tab you are slotting through. Glue or tape the tab in position on the inside.

tab

By using 'split pins' which you can buy in stationery and craft shops, you can make models that move! Try to find a fairly thick but soft card such as old fruit boxes. First decide on the shape of your model and which pieces you want to move.

On our crocodile, the jaw will open and shut and the legs move.

The bird's wings move up and down.

Make a sketch of your model and then cut the pieces out of card. Pierce holes through the parts where the 'joint' will be and push a split pin through. Flatten out the ends of the split pin so that it doesn't fall out. It is easier to paint the pieces of your model before you put the split pins in.

By making simple slits in pieces of card, you will be able to make almost any card shape stand on its own!

Make slits a little wider than a single cut so that the pieces slot together neatly. On one card shape the slit should start at the top and on the other it should start at the bottom. Slits should usually be slightly more than half the height of the shape. The pictures on this page show different methods for slitting and slotting card shapes together.

You can also make a flat piece of card stand up by folding it down the middle.

These pop-up cards are made by cutting and scoring. The main shapes stay attached to the card by tabs. First, mark the centre of a piece of card. Draw the main part of your picture on the lower half of the card. Decide which bits of the picture you want joined. Draw in the tabs. You will need two if it is a big drawing. The length of the tabs should be equal to the distance from the bottom of your drawing to the centre fold. Look at the picture opposite. The blue lines show score lines. Cut and score your picture and tabs and push out from the background.

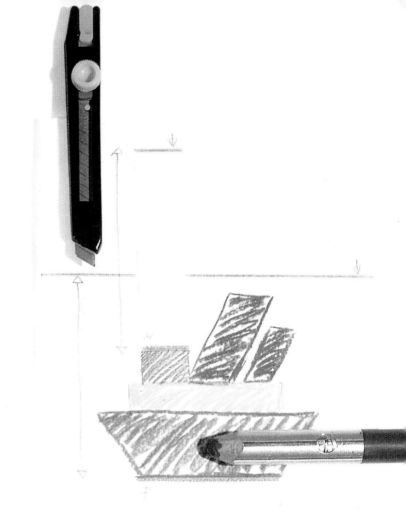

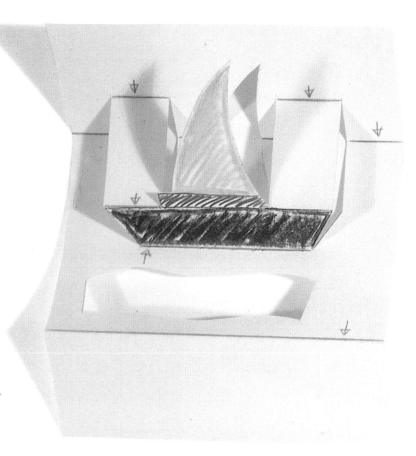

To make your card move, fold under one edge of the card and tape it down to make a pocket. Cut a strip of card slightly longer than the pocket. Pull the strip in and out!

Create your own theatre, actors and scenery from a shoe box and some pieces of card! Invite your friends round and act out your favourite plays with your own characters. On the next two pages you will find out how we made our theatre by slotting in some of the scenery from the top and moving other pieces backwards and forwards from the sides.

Use a shoe box or a fruit box to make the frame for your theatre. Cut a hole at one of the short ends, leaving a narrow frame. Make a decorated front from a piece of thin card and stick it to the frame.

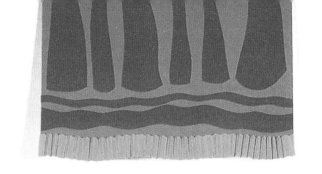

Make a selection of backdrops from pieces of thin card. The backdrops should be slightly higher than the shoe box. Cut slits – about 3 knife cuts wide – so that the backdrops slot comfortably over the box. The distance from the top of the slot to the bottom of the backdrop should be the same height as the box. You can make curtains for your theatre in the same way.

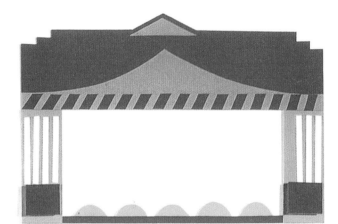

To make characters and props, draw and cut out the shapes, leaving a length of thin card attached. Make slits along the side of the box high enough to push the characters through.

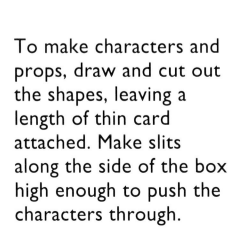

Here are some delicious fruit and vegetables – but they are not for eating! All the examples here are made from papier mâché – a mixture of paste and paper.
On the next page you will find the paste recipe and tips for making the basic framework.

Paste Recipe

1 Measure out a mug of flour and 3 mugs of water.

2 In a saucepan, mix a little of the water with the flour to make a smooth paste.

3 Add the rest of the water and ask a grown-up to heat the mixture until it boils – they must keep stirring all the time! Turn the heat down and let the mixture simmer until the paste thickens.

4 Leave the mixture until it is cold.

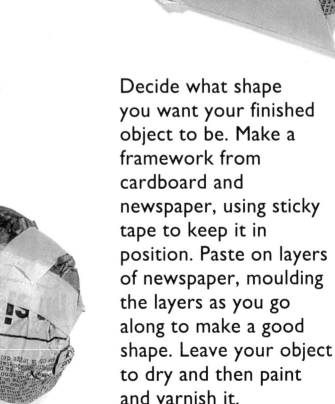

Decide what shape you want your finished object to be. Make a framework from cardboard and newspaper, using sticky tape to keep it in position. Paste on layers of newspaper, moulding the layers as you go along to make a good shape. Leave your object to dry and then paint and varnish it.

MODELS

CONTENTS

All the things on these pages have been used somewhere in the MODELS section. You should be able to find them all at home or at school.

Some modelling material is very sticky and hard to get off certain surfaces, so you should always cover the space you are working in and make sure you ask before using things from around the house.

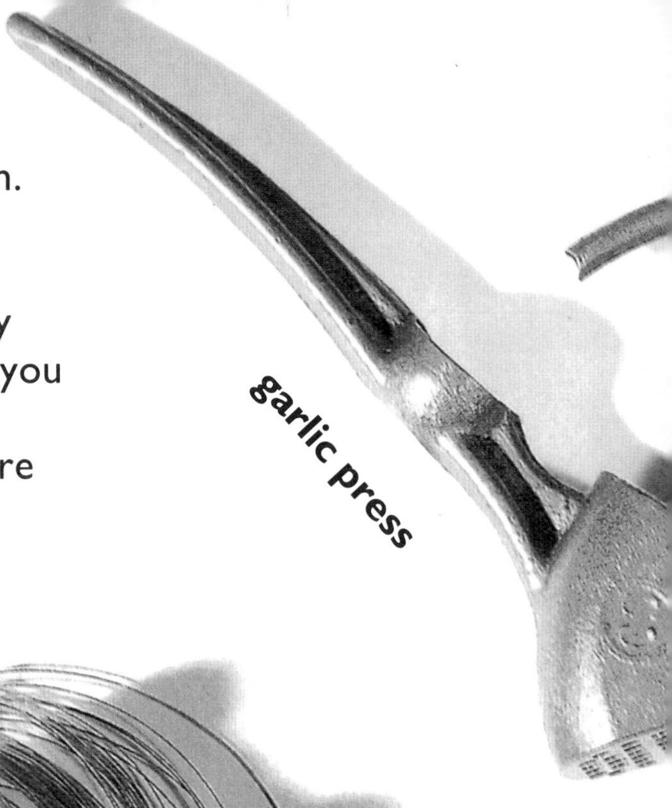

garlic press

fishing twine and wire

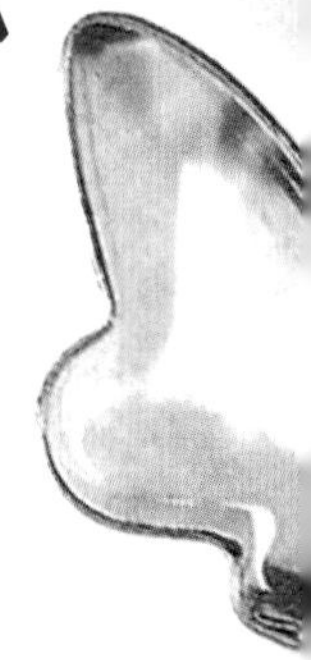

pastry cutters

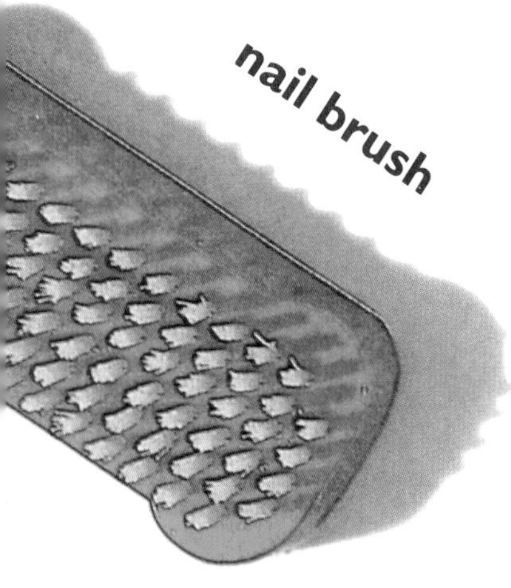

nail brush

cocktail sticks

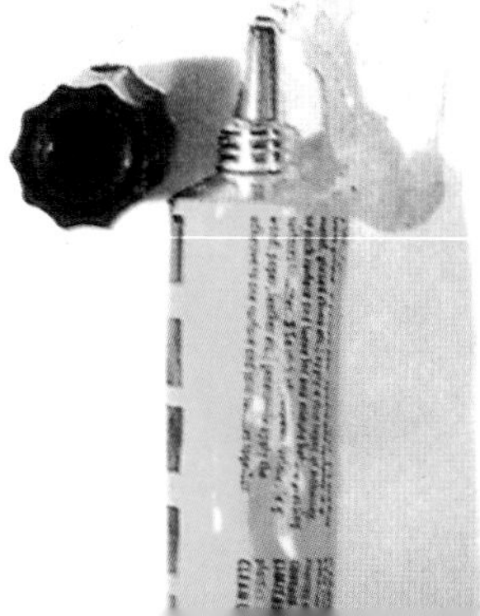

glue

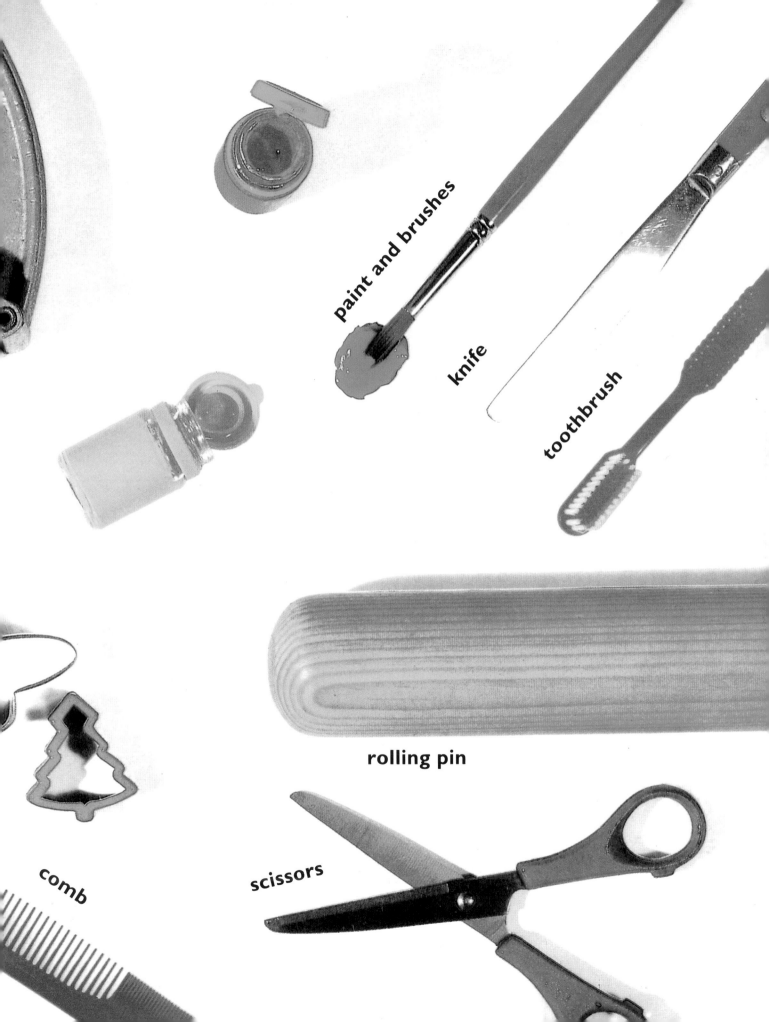

paint and brushes

knife

toothbrush

rolling pin

comb

scissors

Play dough is very easy to make and you can use it again and again. The recipe is on page 116. Press it and roll it into shape and add different colours, or decorate your models with other things, like the fishing twine and sequins which make up these fireworks. Play dough is good for moulding too because it spreads to take on the shape of the container it is put in.

Play dough recipe
300g (12 ounces) flour
115g (4 ounces) salt
225ml (8 fluid ounces) water
2 tablespoons oil
4 tablespoons cream of tartar
food colouring

Mix all the ingredients together then put them in a saucepan. Ask a grown-up to heat it over a low heat, stirring all the time, until it turns into a ball.

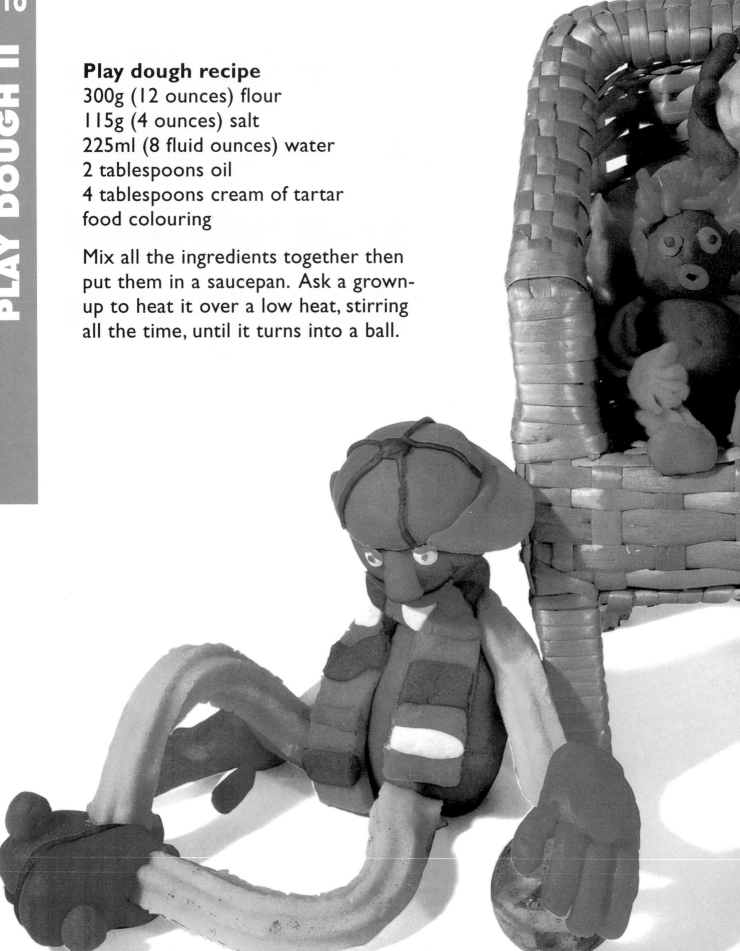

You can use your play dough again
and again as long as you store it in
a sealed container or a plastic bag.

You can make permanent decorations like Christmas ornaments or mobiles with salt dough.

Salt Dough Recipe

225g (8 ounces) plain flour
225g (8 ounces) salt
1 tablespoon wallpaper paste powder
250ml (9 fluid ounces) water

Mix the dry ingredients together and then add the water. Roll the dough out to 5mm (1/4 inch) thickness and then cut out shapes. Make holes in the dough with a cocktail stick so that you can tie ribbons to them when they are dry. Lay on greaseproof paper on a baking sheet and bake for 8 hours in a very cool oven (110°C, 225°F).

   When they are cool the models can be painted with poster paints. Allow the paint to dry before adding two coats of varnish. This seals the dough and stops the decorations from going mouldy.

Non-hardening clay can be modelled over and over again. There are lots of ways to use it – you can join pieces just by pressing them together. Give the clay a marbled effect by rolling two or three different colours into a ball. Use a nail brush or a garlic press to make lots of different shapes and textures.

Making pottery is easier than you imagine! Clay is very cheap and available in most craft shops. If you make mistakes you can always start again.

Try making a pinch pot by pressing your thumb into a ball of clay and gradually hollowing it out. Or make a coil pot by building up long sausages of clay.

Remember to keep your clay covered in plastic or a damp cloth when you are not using it or it will dry out.

Make some slip from left-over fragments of clay soaked in water. Use it to keep the clay you are working on moist and to help stick pieces together. Use an old toothbrush to put the slip on with.

Roll out your clay on a smooth surface and cut out shapes using a knife or cutters.

Make a slab pot by cutting out squares of clay and sticking them to a base. Rub over the joins with lots of slip until they are smooth. You can smooth out your coil pot like this too.

Clay has to be baked in a kiln to make it hard and strong. If you don't have a kiln at school, ask where you can find one in the library or in craft shops.

Decorate your pottery when it is still wet by pressing on shapes or making patterns in the clay. When it has been baked you can paint or varnish it.